DRAWING WITH 4D

DRAWING AIRCRAFT, SHIPS, AND HIGH-SPEED VEHICLES

An Augmented Reading Drawing Experience

BY CLARA CELLA
ILLUSTRATED BY JON WESTWOOD

CAPSTONE PRESS
a capstone imprint

Dabble Lab Books are published by Capstone Press,
1710 Roe Crest Drive, North Mankato, Minnesota 56003
www.mycapstone.com

Library of Congress Cataloging-in-Publication data is available
on the Library of Congress website.
ISBN: 978-1-5435-3188-6 (library binding)
ISBN: 978-1-5435-4235-6 (eBook PDF)

Summary: This book fuels readers' need to draw modes of transportation that move
on land, in the air, and across the sea. Step-by-step instructions and special 4D
components show budding artists how to illustrate airplanes, ships, trucks, and more,
with projects increasing in difficulty to build drawing skills and confidence. Readers
can download the Capstone 4D app for an augmented reality experience that extends
learning beyond the printed page with artist video tutorials and other bonus content.

Editorial Credits
Jill Kalz, editor; Aruna Rangarajan, designer;
Kathy McColley, production specialist

Photo Credits
Capstone Studio: Karon Dubke (yarn art), 30, 31; Shutterstock: Jamen Percy,
5 (pencils and scribbles), Lifestyle Graphic (sheet of paper), cover and throughout,
Little Princess (background pattern), cover and throughout, Mega Pixel, 5 (erasers
and pencil sharpener), Ruslan Ivantsov, 5 (graphite pencil), timquo, 5 (felt marker)

Printed and bound in the USA
PA017

TABLE OF CONTENTS

Download the Capstone app!

- Ask an adult to download the Capstone 4D app.
- Scan the cover and stars inside the book for additional content.

When you scan a spread, you'll find fun extra stuff to go with this book! You can also find these things on the web at www.capstone4D.com using the password: aircraft.31886

HELLO, ARTIST!

Got somewhere to go but don't know how to get there? How about hopping onto a helicopter? Burning rubber in a muscle car? Cruising on a ship? Ten kinds of vehicles are fueled up and ready for you (and your pencil). Pick your favorite!

Easier drawing projects are toward the front of the book. Tougher ones are toward the back. Take one step at a time and practice, practice, practice. Scan the star targets if your drawing starts flying, rolling, or sailing off course. Your 4D instructor will help you get

BACK ON TRACK.

Tools and Supplies

Before you begin your drawing projects,
gather the following tools and supplies:

PAPER

Any type of blank, unlined paper will do.

PENCILS

Pencils are the easiest to use.
Make sure you have plenty of them.

SHARPENER

You'll need clean lines, so keep
a pencil sharpener close by.

ERASER

Pencil erasers wear out very quickly.
Get a rubber or kneaded eraser.

DARK PEN/MARKER

When your drawing is finished, you can
trace over it with a black ink pen or a thin
felt-tip marker. The dark lines will really
make your work pop.

COLORED PENCILS

If you decide to color your drawings,
colored pencils usually work best.

SUBMARINE

The specs for this ballistic missile submarine sound made up, But they're not! The sub is almost two football fields long and as wide as a three-lane highway. It can sail deeper than 800 feet (244 meters). It carries about 150 sailors for months at a time. And it makes oxygen for the crew too.

STEP 1

STEP 2

STEP 3

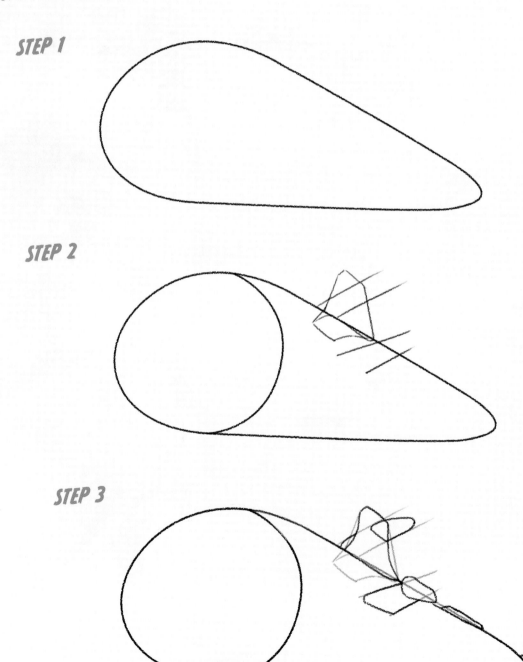

With what sorts of creatures does your sub share the sea? Whales? Giant jellyfish? Great white sharks? Draw them!

STEP 4

STEP 5

FIGHTER JET

By the time you hear this jet, it's gone! Jet speeds are often measured in Mach numbers. Mach 1 is equal to the speed of sound in air. How fast is that? When the air temperature is 70 degrees Fahrenheit (21 degrees Celsius), the speed of sound is about 770 miles (1,239 kilometers) per hour!

STEP 1

STEP 2

STEP 3

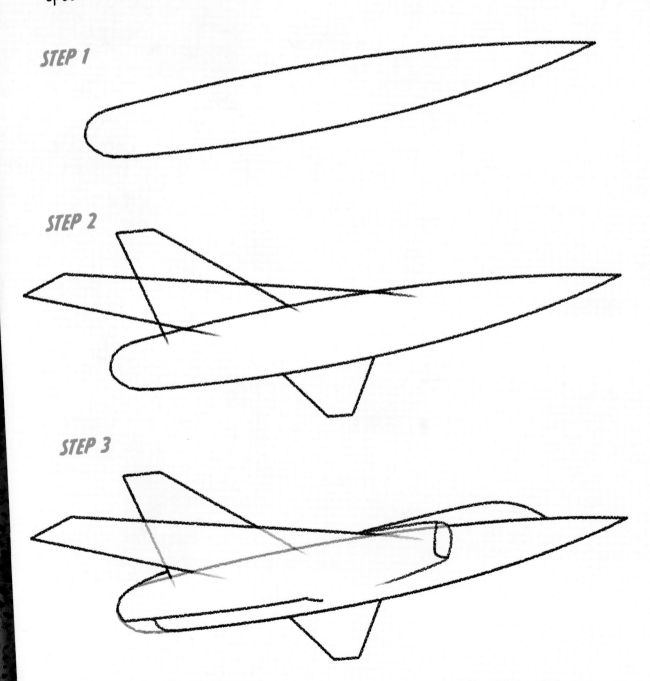

STEP 4

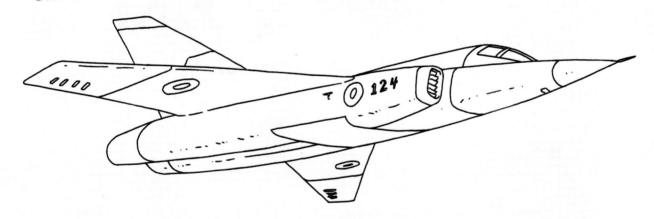

STEP 5

Add two more jets to your drawing to create a V-shaped formation (pattern) called a Vic.

CRUISE SHIP

Unlike *Titanic*, which sank in the Atlantic Ocean in 1912, *this* cruise ship sails safely past the icebergs. Today's cruise ships are like cities on the water. They have restaurants, shops, movie theaters, pools, fitness centers, and more. The largest ships can carry nearly 7,000 passengers!

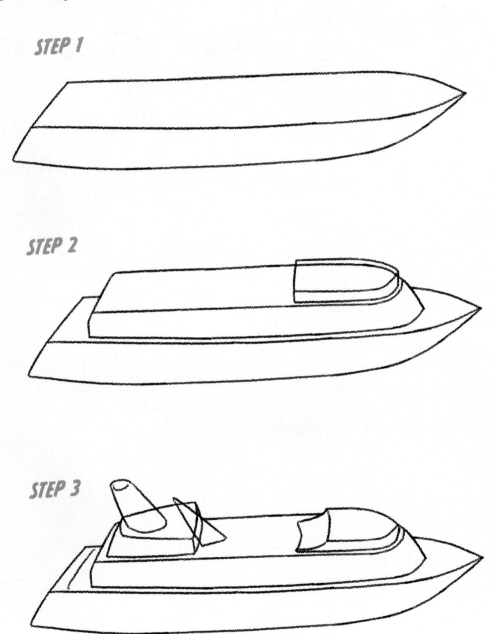

STEP 1

STEP 2

STEP 3

STEP 4

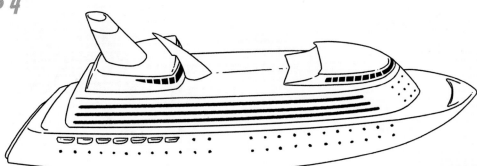

Draw your ship pulling into a port (a town or city along the water).

STEP 5

BIPLANE

The biplane is named for its two sets of fixed wings—*bi* meaning "two." It's probably best known for its use during World War I (1914–1918). A type of British biplane called the Sopwith Camel was especially famous. No airplane shot down more German aircraft than it did.

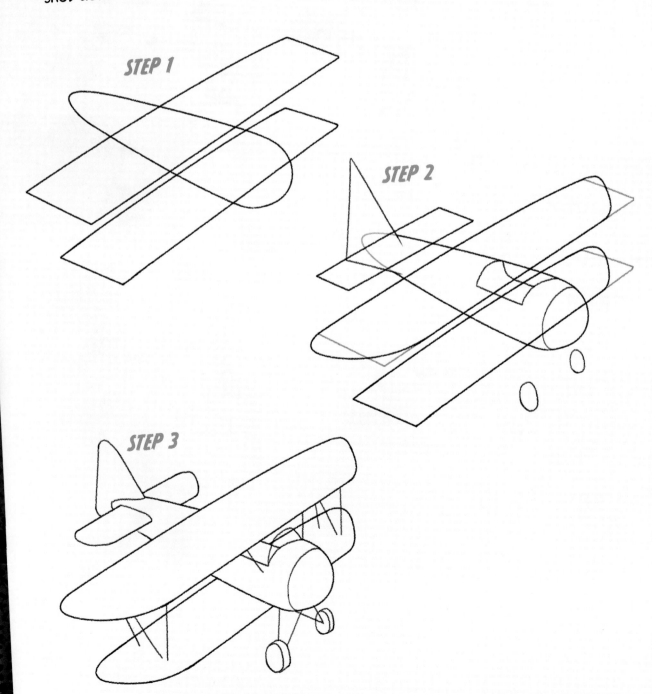

STEP 1

STEP 2

STEP 3

STEP 4

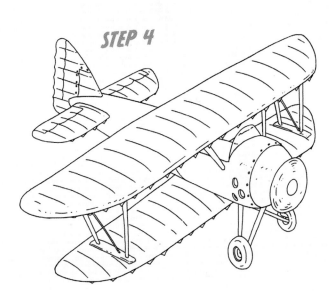

Today, biplanes are often used for air-show stunts (aerobatics). Try drawing your plane doing a smoky loop or corkscrew.

STEP 5

MONSTER TRUCK

If you like big, nasty-looking vehicles, look no further. With an ear-busting roar and ridiculously huge tires, this monster truck crushes anything in its path. Average monster truck tires measure 66 inches (168 centimeters) tall. But a truck called Bigfoot 5 set a world record. Its beastly rubber donuts measured 120 INCHES (305 CM) tall!

STEP 1

STEP 2

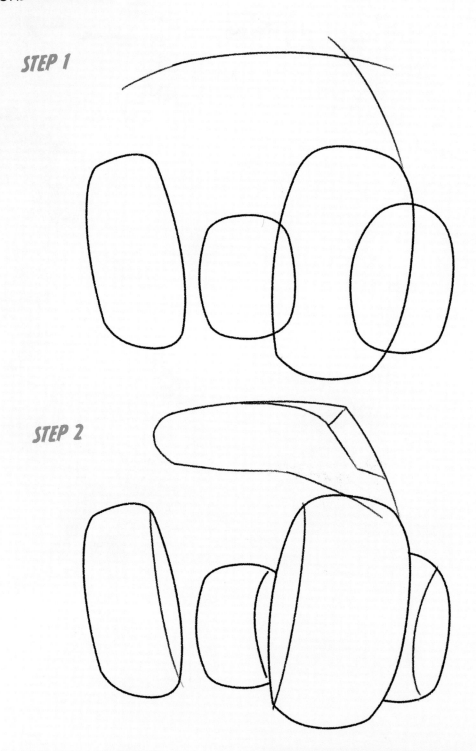

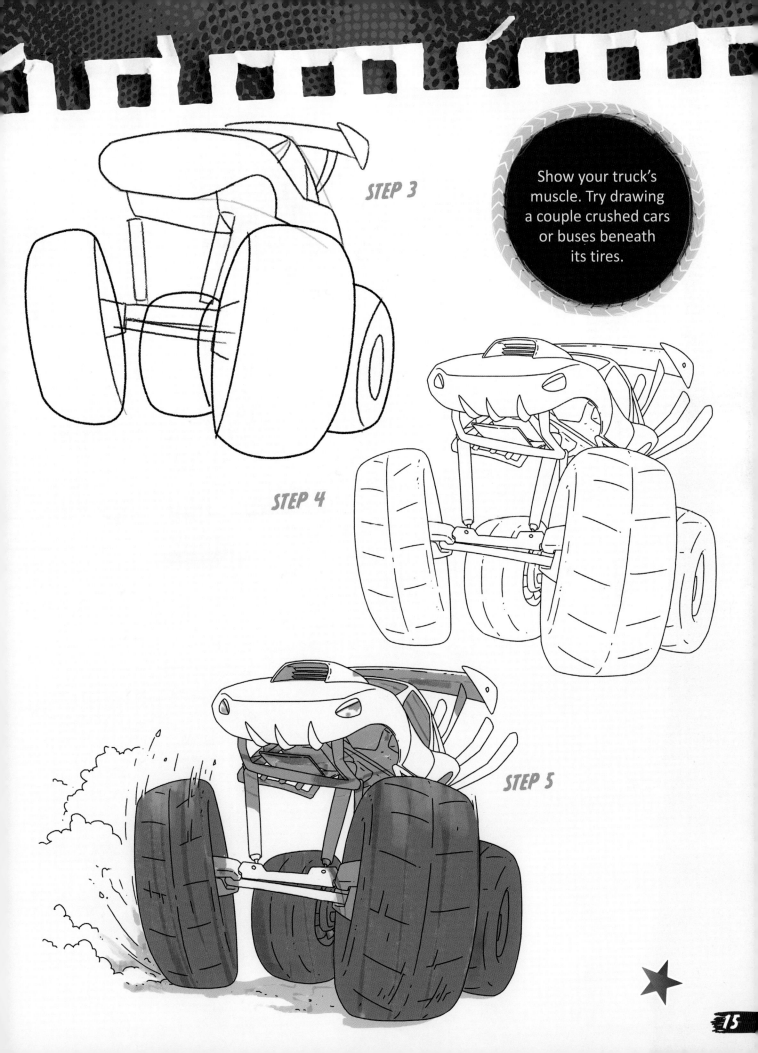

STEP 3

Show your truck's muscle. Try drawing a couple crushed cars or buses beneath its tires.

STEP 4

STEP 5

HELICOPTER

Have to get to a hard-to-reach place, fast? Call in a helicopter! From rescues in the mountains to rescues at sea, helicopters have a long history of saving the day. Why? They need little space (or time) for taking off and landing. They can hover in place. And they move fast over distances.

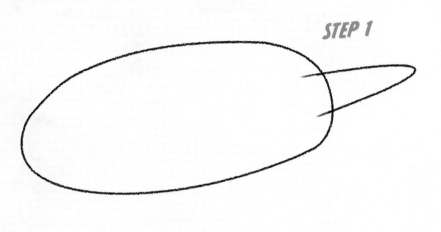

STEP 1

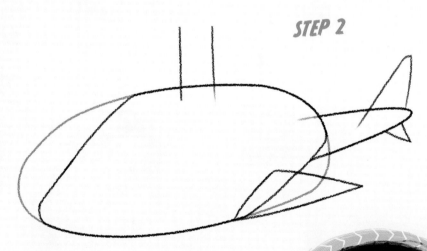

STEP 2

Draw a rescue scene for your helicopter. Is it in a big city? A canyon? A tropical island?

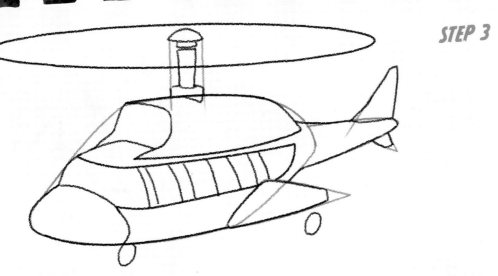

STEP 3

STEP 4

STEP 5

TALL SHIP

Before ships had engines powered by steam or gas, they used the wind. Sailors attached, or rigged, fabric sails to poles called masts. Pirates loved ships like this two-masted, square-rigged beauty. Called a brig, the ship moved quickly—perfect for attacking and looting other ships.

STEP 1

STEP 2

STEP 3

What lies in the waters beneath your ship? Draw a giant octopus or your own imaginary sea monster.

STEP 4

STEP 5

MUSCLE CAR

Hear that growl? That deep rumble? A muscle car is coming! Muscle cars get their name from their powerful, high-performance engines. They first hit the streets in the 1960s and 1970s. Some of the meanest machines included the Pontiac GTO, the Chevy Camaro, and the Shelby Mustang.

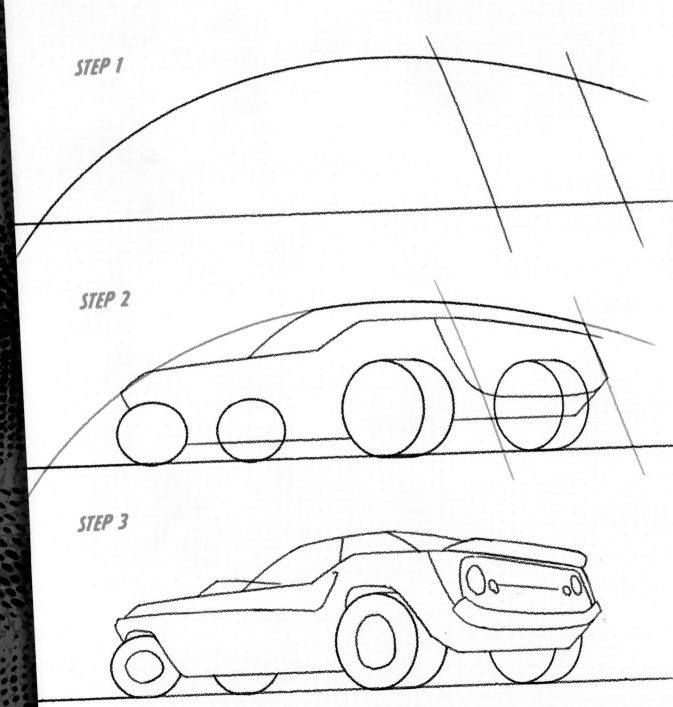

STEP 1

STEP 2

STEP 3

STEP 4

STEP 5

After you've finished drawing your car, give it a custom paint job. Add stripes, flames, or lightning bolts.

MOTORCYCLE

One of the coolest kinds of motorcycles is the leaning three-wheeler. It's also called a reverse trike. With two wheels in front and one in back, this bike loves to hug the road. It leans into curves just like a two-wheel motorcycle, but with better balance. And its rocket-like power leaves other bikes in the dust.

STEP 1

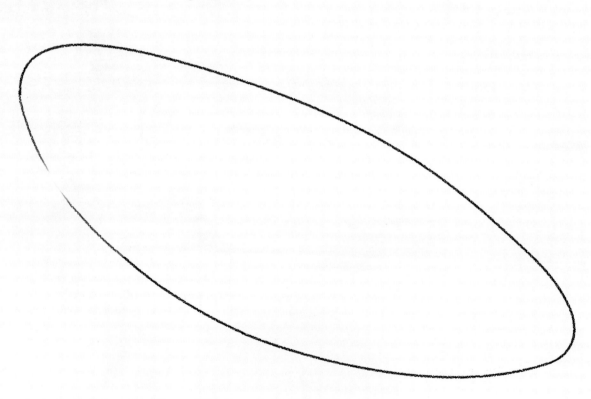

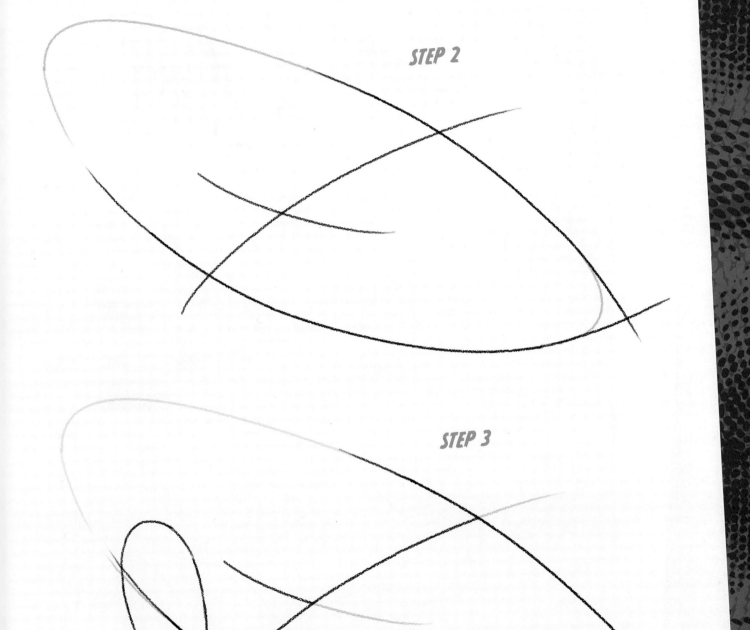

STEP 2

STEP 3

CONTINUED...

STEP 4

STEP 5

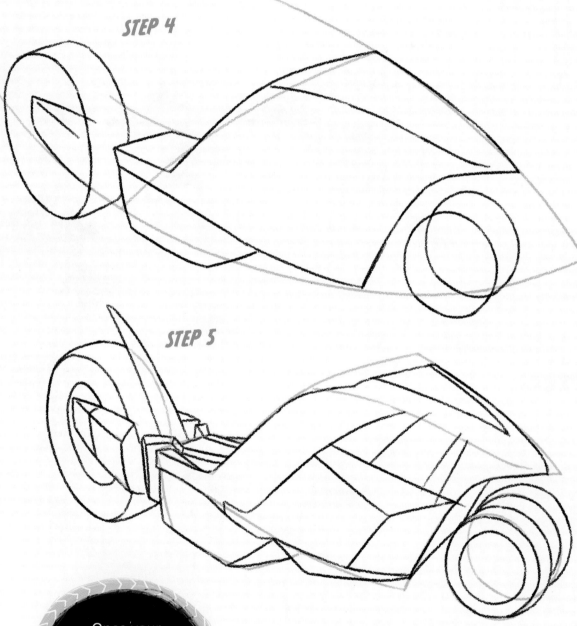

Once your
motorcycle
is done, draw
yourself riding it.
Don't forget
a helmet!

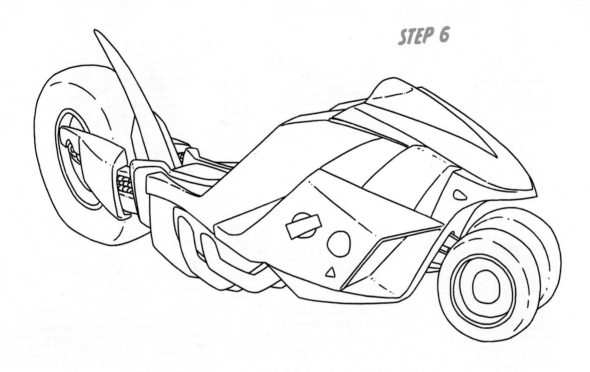

STEP 6

STEP 7

RACE CAR

Tires squeal. Clouds of white smoke rise into the air. In just six seconds, this race car goes from 0 to 250 miles (402 km) per hour. ZOOM! A sloping front end helps reduce drag, the force that pushes against all moving objects and tries to slow them down. Less drag equals more speed.

STEP 1

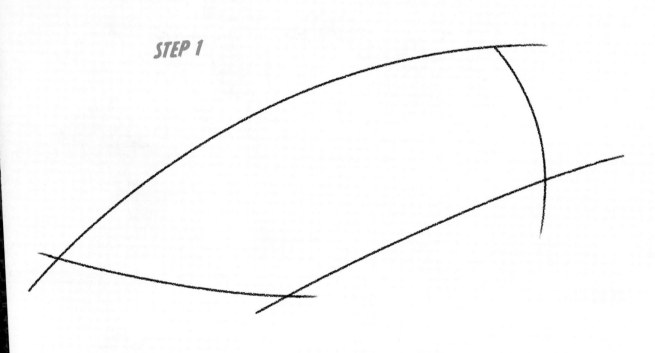

STEP 2

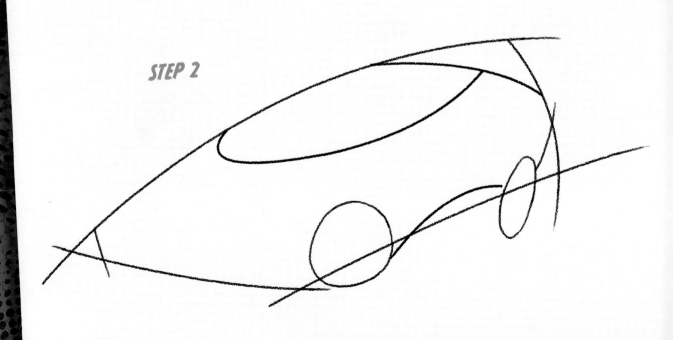

STEP 3

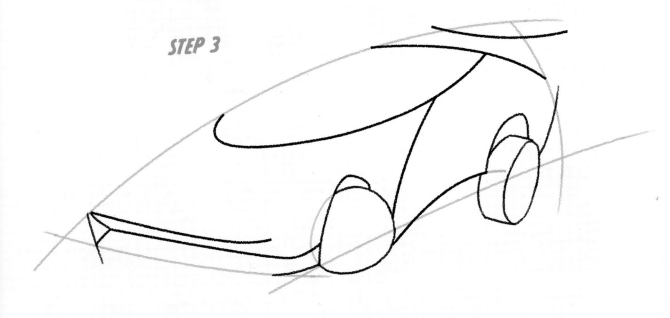

STEP 4

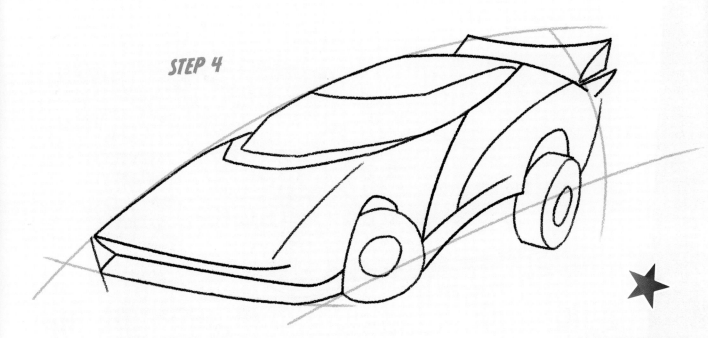

CONTINUED...

STEP 5

STEP 6

It's more fun to race against someone. Draw a few more cars on the track.

STEP 7

CRAFT IT UP!

SOME RIDE, HUH? Well, stay buckled in, because the ride isn't over! Let's take one of your drawings and do something with it. Craft it up!

VEHICLE YARN ART

WHAT YOU NEED:

- a drawing of your favorite vehicle*
- a piece of plywood slightly bigger than your drawing
- a craft mat or other work surface covering
- clear tape
- linoleum nails
- a hammer
- yarn, in multiple colors
- scissors

STEP 1 Lay the plywood board on the craft mat and tape your drawing to the board.

STEP 2 Following the lines of your drawing, lightly pound the nails into the board. Nails should be evenly spaced and hammered to an even depth. Be careful not to pound them all the way through the board!

* An image that fills a standard sheet of paper is best.

STEP 3 Once you're done outlining your drawing with nails, remove the paper.

STEP 4 Choose a yarn color and knot an end around a nail. Keeping the yarn tight, wrap it around a second nail, then a third, then a fourth.

STEP 5 Continue wrapping the yarn from nail to nail, top to bottom, bottom to top. Be sure to keep the yarn tight at all times.

STEP 6 When you're finished with a color section, cut the yarn and knot the end around a nail. Trim any yarn tails.

STEP 7 Repeat steps 4, 5, and 6 with additional colors until all the nails have been wrapped and all the sections are filled with yarn.

Vehicle Yarn Art, ready for takeoff!

READ MORE

Bolte, Mari. *Draw Wild Robot Mash-Ups.* Drawing Mash-Ups. North Mankato, Minn.: Capstone Press, a Capstone imprint, 2018.

Johnson, Clare. *How to Draw.* New York: Dorling Kindersley Limited, 2017.

McCurry, Kristen. *How to Draw Amazing Airplanes and Spacecraft.* Smithsonian Drawing Books. Mankato, Minn.: Capstone Press, 2013.

INTERNET SITES

Use FactHound to find Internet sites related to this book:

Visit *www.facthound.com*

Just type in 9781543531886 and go.

MAKERSPACE TIPS

Download tips and tricks for using this book and others in a library makerspace.

Visit *www.capstonepub.com/dabblelabresources*